JOY MINTER PRESENTS

ROUGH TRADE

Katie Pollock

CURRENCY PRESS
The performing arts publisher

CURRENT THEATRE SERIES

First published in 2022
by Currency Press Pty Ltd,
PO Box 2287, Strawberry Hills, NSW, 2012, Australia
enquiries@currency.com.au
www.currency.com.au

in association with Joy Minter.

Typeset by Brighton Gray for Currency Press.
Cover features Katie Pollock; image by Teniola Komolafe.
Cover design by Emma Bennetts.

Currency Press acknowledges the Traditional Owners of the Country on which
we live and work. We pay our respects to all Aboriginal and Torres Strait
Islander Elders, past and present.

A catalogue record for this
book is available from the
NATIONAL LIBRARY
OF AUSTRALIA
National Library of Australia

Contents

ACKNOWLEDGEMENTS

I acknowledge the Gadigal people of the Eora nation, traditional custodians of the land on which this work was written and produced, and pay my respects to their elders past, present and emerging. Always was, always will be, Aboriginal land.

This work was written and produced with the assistance of Inner West Council, Sydney Fringe Festival, City of Sydney and, most importantly, the humans of Rough Trade Sydney. The members and moderators of the Rough Trade community have my undying thanks.

Rough Trade was first produced by Joy Minter, in association with Sydney Fringe Festival, at the Seymour Centre, Sydney, on 6 September 2022, with the following cast:

WOMAN	Katie Pollock

Director, Anthony Skuse
Lighting Design, James Wallis
Sound Design, Cluny Edwards
Stage Manager, Maya Soni
Assistant Producer, Tabitha Woo

CHARACTERS

A WOMAN in her 50s or 60s. She might be you. Or me. Or one of us in a few years' time … someone who definitely didn't expect to be where she is at this point in her life.

SETTING

The stage. An imaginative space with minimal set. No sofas, no beds, no boring.

There is a child's chair onstage, and a few boxes.

TIME

One day in the Inner West.

NOTES

Tomorrow is not yet written.

This play text went to press before the end of rehearsals and may differ from the play as performed.

ONE: SLUGS

A WOMAN *sits on a child's chair—one of those old wooden ones that's rather beautiful, but still, a chair meant for a child, not a woman of a certain age.*

There are a few cardboard boxes onstage. She has a mobile phone.

She talks directly to the audience.

WOMAN: You probably came here expecting to see a show about sex. Right?
I've got some bad news—it's actually a show about slugs.

I know. Totally understand if you want to leave now …

But before you go, there is one little fact about slugs you might want to hear—
they're hermaphrodites.
Meaning both sexual organs are contained in the same individual.

It's very inner west.

They're like, fuck you latecomers, we've been nailing this gig for five hundred and twenty million years!

The thing is, even though they don't have to, most slugs do choose to mate.
And when they do,
it's actually pretty spectacular.
I looked it up because … well, bear with me.

The slugs hang themselves from a mucus rope,
roll around each other like overcooked fusilli,
then both push out a giant penis from the side of their heads and jizz out some sperm.
And with the sperm they fertilise the other slug's eggs or they eat it for lunch.
So … options!
And the best part is,

if they're not in the mood to mingle,
they can literally go fuck themselves.

There's a YouTube on it that goes for about five minutes. Somebody
    filmed slug sex. And at first you're like okay, yeah, cool … in a
    science-y kinda way?
Then you're like whoa!
What the—?!
Ew!
Get that thing away from me!

It was exhausting.
After a couple of minutes, I had to pull out.
You can't see who's coming where, and the plot is terrible,
but hey, slug porn—
what do you expect?

Before the slugs took over,
back when I thought I was doing a show about sex,
I imagined it would be a musical
and there would be singing, dancing dildos
high-kicking across the back of the stage.
All the joy!
All the glamour!

   She pictures them, gestures.

Lovely.

Unfortunately nobody answered my callout for extras willing to
    prance around dressed as an enormous phallus …
which means gastropod erotica is the closest we're going to get to
    a chorus line.

***

So I'm standing in the garden
and I see this shimmer in the corner where the rats usually hang out.
It looks pretty,
until I realise what it is.

The silvery trail leads my eye across the concrete
and there, glistening among the weeds, is …
the slug.

I nudge the foliage aside with my shoe,
look closer.
There, next to the slug, is its partner in slime—
let's call them 'Slugella'.
And next to Slugella is their bestie, 'Slugfried',
and there's their fuck buddy 'Slugbert',
and *their* kink buddy 'Slugena'.
Loads of them.

   She stands on the chair.

They've slugged all over the deck,
and now they're just sitting there,
like tiny malevolent poos,
waiting for nightfall
so they can squeeze in
and rampage around the kitchen.
Slimy fuckers.

I just don't see the point of them.

Someone said to try getting rid of them with beer.
It's kryptonite to slugs.
You fill up a bowl, they drink, they drown, you dispose of the
   bodies.

Now,
you may have noticed I am a woman of a certain age,
and therefore enraged at the world and want to smash a lot of things.
But I'm not a murderer.

So I have a garden full of slugs.
There is no frickin' way I'm picking them up.
And no matter how kinky and cool their sex life is,
I just want someone else to deal with them.

What do I do?

I put out a call on Rough Trade.

TWO: ROUGH TRADE

WOMAN: Rough Trade is my favourite Facebook group.

Don't laugh—
it actually took me a while before I found out there was more than
  one meaning to Rough Trade.
For those of us here who have lived life on the more manicured side
  of the tracks,
I'm not referring to the Canadian art punk band or late seventies
  record label.

Others can explain it better than me.

This is from the Oxford Dictionary:

She reads from her phone.

> Rough trade:
> a tough or sadistic element among male homosexuals.

> And here's the Cambridge:
> Male prostitutes who have sex with other men
> and who give the appearance of being from a poor social class.

Goodness.

Her phone pings.

Ooh! Hang on.

She checks it.

For the avoidance of doubt, this is not a male prostitute.

Alas.

It's the latest listings in the group:

> Pet door still embedded in an actual door …
> platform boots …

eight-kilo bag of rice with bonus weevils …
a thimble with the Pope on it …
left-over condoms …
parrot feathers for craft or kinky times …
a half-used bottle of soy sauce …

Peak Rough Trade.

Beat.

Let us first agree that Facebook is evil.
A multinational corporation that pays miniscule taxes,
monetises anger,
spies on you and sells your information to any bidder,
including those people selling period undies and incontinence pads.
What is with all those fucking ads?
I can't be in BOTH demographics!

But …

It's also a place of connection and celebration,
sometimes tipping over into boasting, sure,
but really you should be happy about that friend's success *okay*?
And it's a place to offload stuff—
the flotsam and jetsam masquerading as your life.

Rough Trade is one of those quirky Facebook groups that's sprung
     up in our little corner of the internet.
It's like Marketplace but money is strictly forbidden,
so people swap or trade things.
Simple.
Take a second and think of the most ridiculous, outlandish thing
     you could possibly put up for trade …
Done it?
I guarantee someone on Rough Trade wants that thing.

If it's weird and eccentric it's good …
if it's sexy and bad,
it's great.

Before you rush to sign up I must warn you,
this is a private group.
You have to ask to be let in,
which means you can be chucked out …
because there are RULES.
Along with no money, no unsolicited advice, and no animals
(except for the infamous goat exchange),
is rule nine,
don't be a dick:

She reads from her phone.

> No bigotry tolerated here. This is a group for raging lefties.
> Check that intolerant nonsense at the door or you will get
> mercilessly ridiculed and probably booted.

Trust me,
you don't want to mess with that shit.
I've seen it happen
and it takes a lot of scrubbing to get the stains off the walls.

Mostly it's kooky, often kinky, and always interesting.

She reads from her phone.

> Three right arms and three left legs. Medical models. Two
> kilos each. Trade for a lemon.

Tempting, right?
It's filled with these little moments.
Picture it:
two strangers meet on a doorstep,
a leg under each arm …

Trading isn't about the intrinsic value of the thing on offer,
it's about perceived equivalence.
What's valuable to you and what's valuable to me are probably not
    the same thing.

You see an old shirt.
I see something that once sat close to my heart
before it expanded out of my chest

brushed past my lover's skin
and melted into his body.

You see a sofa.
I see the place we collapsed,
giggling like children,
beside ourselves with luck and joy at finding each other.

Someone wanted to do a trade once where the respondent would
    clipper the poster's legs and then shave them while the poster
    drank Diet Coke and read a short story aloud.
That's not a thing with a dollar value.

For Roughies,
the word 'money' is almost synonymous with
'insert racist-mysogynist-classist-ablist-homophobic-biphobic-
transphobic slur here'.

Sometimes I'm not sure I belong here,
not sure I'm cool enough.
I'm not young,
I'm not boho,
I don't tick the right boxes …

But I don't belong out there either.
I don't make heaps of money,
I'm not a producer of things.
I'm not 'useful'.
In a value-add society, I'm a value-minus.
I'm a lot of nots.
Sometimes it feels pretty close to not being anything.

Beat.

Her phone pings.

Ooh! Hang on.
The delicious ping.

Hey are you still in slug hell over there? I think I can help.

Brilliant!

As a trade, they want me to polish their hammer.
Totally legit.
I have a side hustle in sharpening and polishing knives.
It's a skill I picked up along the way for …
reasons.
So we're on!

This chick comes over and picks up my slugs, one by one.
She puts them in a plastic container and takes them away.
I could kiss her.

Next day she's up on Rough Trade:

'One box of slugs. Name your trade.'

Someone has a pen full of chickens hungry for fresh meat,
they hand over a few eggs,
the slugs go to meet their maker,
and the deal is done.

Everyone's happy.

THREE: A HOUSE

WOMAN: I'm waiting on a trade.

This one should get me closer to the threshold.
I'm not talking about some mythical hero's journey bullshit.
I mean a literal threshold.
I want a tiny house.

They're all the rage.
Sustainable.
Green.
Small footprint.
But beautiful and perfectly formed.
A bit like this chair, which should fit in fine.
Someone posted up earlier looking for a chair exactly like this,
but I'd have to be desperate to give this up.

This chair has been a safe port in a lava flow.
A throne, and a hurdle.
A cave and an asteroid.

Also the tiny size goes snappily well with my budget.

I used to have money.

I've worked my whole life.
But when you get to a certain age it's … well …
you have the choice of employing a twenty-three-year-old or me,
   who are you going to choose?
Because it doesn't matter how much time I spend online, I wasn't
   raised by the internet,
so I might as well have been raised by wolves.

Fuck,
I bet 'raised by wolves' would actually tick a box somewhere.

Covid's been tough.
I got a job at Coles stacking shelves on the night shift.
It was at the beginning when everyone was going psycho over the
   loo roll.
Apparently there were three hundred applicants for five positions.
I felt great about myself when I got that call.
But jeez it was hard work.
And right after the doomsday preppers settled down, they let the
   new hires go.
Some of us, anyway.

Most places now, they just don't pick me.
And bit by bit the savings drip away.

So I'm on benefits for the first time in my life.
Report in,
mutual obligations,
all that.
Some weeks, after rent and bills, I have fifteen dollars left.
Sometimes a half-used bottle of soy sauce is just the ticket.

If I have to, I use the blessing box
but I don't like going there—
I'd rather leave that for people who really need it.
And there are the Pay-It-Forward pages if you want to act like a
    hungry seagull:
Mine! Mine! Mine!

But I am not a charity case.
I'd rather do trades.

I have multiple Facebook profiles.
It's against the rules—
what Facebook calls its 'community standards'—
but it's much more fun.

Facebook also thought I was going against community standards
    when I tried to trade a couple of old Ikea cabinets:

'Two steel cabinets. I took the legs off one so it sits on top of the
    other but I still have the legs and the screws. Great for storing
    shoes so they don't go mouldy in sweaty Sydney.'

Apparently the heady combo of 'legs', 'sit on top', 'sweaty' and
    'screws'
violated Facebook's rules on overtly sexual products.
So you don't want me to have more than one profile?
Go zuck yourself.

I can be who I want on here.
I can be young,
I can be popular,
I can be visible.

Hell,
I could be a man.

There are incredible stories.
I know of at least two people who got cars through trades.
One of them traded up from a wheel of cheese.

I call it the red paperclip effect.
If Rough Trade was a superhero, the red paperclip would be its
    origin story.
Here it is.

This Canadian guy has one red paperclip that he puts up on
    Craigslist—
that's PRE-Facebook.
I know right?
(Mind blown.)
He trades the paperclip for a fish-shaped pen, which he then trades
    for a doorknob, and that for a camping stove, then a generator,
    a keg of beer, a snowmobile, a trip to British Columbia, a truck,
    a recording contract, a year's free rent, an afternoon with Alice
    Cooper, a KISS-themed snow dome, a role in a Hollywood film,
    and finally he trades the film role for a house.
Essentially he trades a paperclip for a house.

He based his idea on a childhood game called Bigger Better,
    which takes off an ancient Buddhist folktale called The Straw
    Millionaire,
about a pauper who becomes wealthy by trading up from a piece
    of straw.

Red Paperclip Guy said he had no idea where his game would end,
    that it was about
'the people'
and
'the journey'
more than the wins.
But he did end up with a house,
so he's saying that from a pretty comfy spot on the Jason Recliner
    in his own living room.

There's also a version of the story in reverse,
in which a man makes ever worse trades until he's left with nothing
    but is happy to be free of his worldly burdens.

Otherwise known as divorce.

So in the middle of Covid, someone pops up on Rough Trade on a
     quest to trade a bobby pin for a house.
Fed up with doomscrolling, she's seen Paperclip Guy on a Ted Talk
and been inspired to try it herself.

First comment in, a Roughie soft-shames her with a BuzzFeed clip
     about a chick in San Francisco who's doing exactly the same and
     sharing 'her journey' with five million followers.
BuzzFeed Chick says:
'Honestly, I love that it's a bit of an FU to capitalism.'

The Rough Trade crowd goes ballistic.
They're not afraid to use the word fuck in public.
Merciless flaming,
until Bobby Pin slinks off to lick her wounds.

The whole idea goes against the spirit of the group.
Because essentially it buys into the capitalist program of wanting
     more,
instead of being happy with enough.
If the thing you want to trade for has to be
'bigger'
or
'better',
then it is entirely about making a profit off another person's loss.

I hated it, along with everyone else.

But a small part of me thought,
why not me?

Why not?

Just one tiny house …

That's capitalism's great trick, isn't it?
To make itself seem like the natural order of things.
And because we're all raised within the system,

steeped in it like mother's milk,
it's very hard to get the taste for it out of our mouths.

And if you're not winning at capitalism that's *your* failure,
not the failure of a system that was stacked against you from the start.

FOUR: SEX

WOMAN: It would be remiss of me not to talk about sex.
I know, I know what I said,
but it is *rough* trade after all.

And everyone's doing it.
If they're not getting slimy with their kink buddy,
they're getting kinky with themselves.
Or they're damn sure thinking about it.

She reads from her phone.

Unwanted sex toys and bondage gear. I've cleaned the crap
out of any that have been used. And none of them have been
used in the past year anyway, thanks Covid. Trade for a hot
post-Covid date with a soft/hard butch masc babe. Seriously
though can we make a Rough Trade dating group?

I have this fancy vulva-shaped bar of soap in a fancy box.
Trade for a bag of concrete.

Vegan paddle that leaves a cute heart. Trade for a Bonsoy?

Looking for dildos! As many as I can collect. Preference is
for the rubbery/silicone type that will wobble through the
air as we fling them out of our trebuchet.

Glorious vag pillow, gifted from my thesis supervisor. Yes,
you can stick your hand in the silky bit.

Old-school leather studded collars in pristine condition.
Trade for berries, bananas or baking mixes. I think this tells
you everything you need to know about the trajectory my
life has taken.

Do you love fisting? My ex convinced me to buy this
novelty dildo, it's about thirty centimetres long and nine
centimetres wide at the knuckles. Some slight discolouration
on the back (see pics).

Beginners' party pack of dildos. The biggest toy—a legit
bad dragon—has some friction burn. By the way, the dragon
is bigger than it looks—picture of my arm for comparison.

Gee, I wish I'd got the slide projector working for this part of the show …

If any of the above offends your delicate sensibilities you're in the
    wrong place.
Just scroll on past.
I love it.
I've learned so much.

Which brings me to today's big trade:
I have a senserator double pro.
It's a sex toy that has a little vacuum part on the top that sucks on
    your clit while the 'double' section services your *other* needs.
They're very popular.
Also butt plugs.
People love those.

I'm asking to trade the senserator double pro for a grocery voucher.
Vouchers are skating perilously close to actual money
but you don't pull out the big guns unless you really need them.
I've been hanging on to the senserator for a while.
And it's lovely to ask people to name their trade,
but I've got enough plant cuttings to start turning back climate
    change in Marrickville West and these things are worth a bomb.

I'm also going to insist on trading in person.

It's not a come-on.
I like to talk to people.

During the first lockdown it was just me and the cat,
and the one-sided conversation did my head in.

I like a stroke as much as the next gal,
but it's nice to be offered a cup of tea and a bit of chat after.

In the thick of that first wave
the moderators suspended trading for safety.
Before we'd worked out contactless, and masks, and vaccines.
Remember that,
when we were all so scared?
Scared of The Thing, and scared of each other.
Well, there are some things more scary than Covid.

I collect cardboard boxes for the same reason.

Someone's always moving
and you can get a whole life story out of a stack of cardboard.
Besides, you never know who might be into something outlandish
    involving bubble wrap and a tape gun.

Women my age aren't supposed to talk about sex,
and we're definitely not supposed to like it.
It's the shame factor.
The visuals.
All those wrinkly bits and wobbly bits crashing into each other.
I can see you squirming in your seats even now.
Low-level coughing.
Teeth gnashing.

We're like a cheese fondue set from the late seventies.
Delicious at the time,
but the parts got rusty and now we're more hassle than we're worth.

It's totally different for men.
Fine for a sixty-year-old bloke to ogle a young woman across the
    dinner table.
Poor fella, he can't help it—
She's beautiful!

I don't want to be looked at *like that*.
But I do want to be looked at.

Pretend I'm still a human being.
Be seen.

I don't recall the precise moment I became invisible.
It's a cloak that slowly wraps itself around you,
first a grateful jacket on a winter morning,
later a suffocating blanket on a humid night.
a stained rug in a burning house.

The focus shifts,
sharpens onto something else,
and suddenly you find yourself blurred out of the picture.
You're something to rush past,
like a stained rug in a burning house.

I'm considering going on a crime spree just to see if anyone notices.

My mother-in-law got caught shoplifting once,
when she was about my age.
She'd stolen a tin of baked beans.
When they asked her why she'd done it, all she could come up with
	was:
'Things are so expensive these days.'

I can feel that tin of beans,
the cold metal edge of it slipping through her fingers into the bag.

I want to feel the edges of my skin again.

And nobody on Rough Trade is going to shame me for exploring
	those edges.

I traded a terrarium for a vibrator once and it was the best thing
	ever.
Then I traded the vibrator for a pair of roller skates and I've never
	lived a better life.

There's a feeling of completeness when you get a really great trade.
Almost … orgasmic.
It's that old capitalist milkman rattling his bottles.

I want things.
I know sometimes I'm just filling the hole,
but it doesn't stop me wanting them all the same.

I have a list of trades currently in play.
Okay, it's a spreadsheet …
what I've got on offer,
what they're offering me,
when and where to meet,
how many messages back and forth,
because sometimes you're like enough already!
I've given you four chances to turn up and you've rearranged
    each one? I get it, shit happens, but if this was Tinder you'd be
    ghosted by last week.

It's only fair.
You try lugging shit around this city on public transport.

That's one of my biggest regrets, not getting my driver's licence.
Not because of the schlepping,
because then at least,

if it all goes bung,

at least I could sleep in my car.

I had to give up my place after I lost the Coles job,
rents are …
criminal, I think the word is …
and this was all I could get.
They wouldn't let me bring the cat.
I actually miss the conversation.
But half the residents here are mad and the other half are high,
so now when I talk to myself I fit in fine.

Just have to keep the knives sharp.

The upside is everyone is too out of it to notice the lemon tree
    poking out of the weeds in this thing that passes for a garden.
Lemons are top currency.

So I have an endless supply of citric loot,
and people love a good squeeze.

If that gets me a spanking horse or some natty little restraining cuffs
    that you need out of your life because they were left behind by
    your narcissistic alcoholic abusive ex-boyfriend,
I don't call that a rough trade,
I call it very very smooth.

FIVE: ZUCKED

WOMAN: Funny how taking stuff away might be the best gift you can
    give someone.

But I have a soft spot for people who need things.
Want things.
It feels like they're more alive somehow,
moving forwards.

I know—capitalism.

Still,
ISO is my favourite.

This is Rough Trade language:
NYT means name your trade.
NTN is no trade needed.
LOOP is listed on other pages.
NIL is next in line,
PIF is pay it forward and
ISO is in search of.

Every time I do a trade with someone I get them into a chat
and try and find out what their thing is.
What it is they really want.
And they tell me.
Maybe nobody ever asked them that before—
what are you in search of?

I write all their answers on my spreadsheet, in case I come across
    something, and then I can go:
Hey,
weren't you looking for a penguin head a while back?
So-and-so just posted one up,
take a look.
I'm a matchmaking service for weird shit.

And people are looking for all kinds of things.
Basic goods, you know—
A cat backpack.
A tortoise costume.
Nipple pasties.
People with hidden talents.
Lightening someone's load.
A life not clouded by drugs.
Making people smile.
A community that's exactly what I needed when I was a teenager
    and feeling isolated and alone.
A real place.
I'm in search of myself.

Do they think they'll find their thing on Rough Trade?
Yes.
Always yes.

Need advice on finding a queer-friendly psychologist with
    experience of adult ADHD diagnosis?
You're in the right place.

Or what about the lesbian couple looking for a sperm donor with
    geographically specific First Nations heritage?
A Rough Trade baby!
Cute!

Or maybe you have no working rights or Medicare card,
you're out of your anxiety meds
and you're spiralling fast.

This is where Rough Trade moves into a whole different orbit.
In search of XYZ …
relief, respite, a way to stop the noise.
Please send help.

Ask for whatever you want,
you'll get no judgement from me.
Just remember—

> *Snap blackout.*

[*In darkness*] Oh crap.

Hello?

What's going on …
Is there a …?

> *Her phone pings. A tiny light comes on.*

> Yo yo hello! Did you hear? Rough Trade got zucked.

Arseholes!

Yep, we got smashed for not following 'community standards'.
Shut down.
Dead.

> *Her phone pings.*

And then another little message.
Like a whisper.

'There's a shadow group.'

> *The lights come back on in full.*

And we're back.
Rougher and tradier, but same rules, same love.
And we're all messaging everyone we ever traded with:
join the new group, sign up, sign up.

Pretty soon the memes are back.

'Facebook sucks. It's for old people … That's because your friends
     aren't gay communists!'

And a warning from the mods:

'Don't be blatant fucking idiots and put this group at risk again.
   Thanks, love you all.'

   Beat.

It was a shock.
We lost over nine thousand members with one click of the mouse.
You think you have control over something but you don't.
We exist at the sufferance of others
and it is a fragile peace.
A delicate necklace of connections.

Did somebody report us?
Who knows …

And what about all the trades in play? All the people?
Gone.

   Her phone pings.

Ooh!
Hang on.

Obviously you think I'm addicted to the notifications.
Correct.
Because what if I miss the perfect trade?

   It pings again. She glances at it.

Ha ha! See?!
The senserator is live and people are into it.
Or it's into them.
Woo hoo!

These high-tech toys are popular.
Everyone's over dating apps.
Bumble's for fakes.
Hinge is for people who live in Woop Woop
and Tinder is full of psychos who want to stick their tongue down
   your throat before you can say a glass of rosé please.

Slugs and humans—not so different.
Trust me,
self-love is the new cheese fondue.

Okay, let's see who's keen.

Checks her phone. Scrolling ... scrolling ...

Hmm.
That's odd.

There's a million hearts and next in lines,
but no grocery vouchers mentioned and no, I didn't ask for a frickin'
  plant cutting and where are the trades?!

Oh my god.
No way ...

I can't believe you're making this NTN.

This is not no trade needed,
it's grocery vouchers!

I don't understand ...
The post said ...
[*Checking her phone*] Oh Jesus ...
'Grocery voucher or NTN.'

Oh that's humiliating.

I'll look like an arsehole if I change it now.

Okay, okay,
give me a second.

She types into her phone.

Edit: I am an arsehole. When I wrote NTN my fingers must
have been possessed by some rich bastard who doesn't have
tumbleweed blowing through their fridge and three days
until their next Centrelink payment. I meant to write trade
for a grocery voucher or *NYT* ...

[*To audience*] In case anyone has a better idea for …
you know …
food.

       [*Typing*] I'm so sorry.
Save.
   Rethinks.
Fuck.
   Types into her phone again.

       Edit on the edit: If you are also struggling right now and
       really need this in your life then … NTN.

Save.

Fuck.

I hate fucking up.

It *can* be kind of terrifying on there.
Bobby Pin Girl haunts my dreams sometimes.

Because if I get chucked off the page then …

Just remember the rule:
don't be a dick.
Don't be a dick and someone will have your back.

Maybe some of the NILs didn't read it too closely?

Next in line is really a desperate fling of hope into the outer reaches
    of the internet.
You're praying that someone else fails to front up for their trade—
thus behaving like the arsehole you know yourself *not* to be—
so that you can step into the breach
and claim what's rightfully yours.

But one of the rules of the group is that the poster doesn't have to
    trade with the first to comment,

or even the next in line.
They get to pick what trade they like best.

In a group full of radical leftie pinko commies,
that's as much power as you're allowed to wield.

You can NIL a hundred things and never get to the top of the line.
So don't be judgy on my notifications.

I'm hungry.
But I'm not an arsehole.

How is it the world turns and turns and then suddenly seems to turn
  the wrong way?

SIX: BREAK-UPS

WOMAN: Break-ups are huge.
  Mass offloading of goods,
  often top quality,
  but blazing with emotional energy.

  Objects hold meaning for people,
  of course they do.
  Memories get stuck,
  bound into the fabric of things,
  tethering them to the past.

  It makes sense, right?
  This is just a chair,
  a few sticks of wood,
  but it's also atoms moving around
  so it's not really solid at all, there are spaces in between.

  There's something about the potential energy stored in the
      arrangement of parts,
  and the power required to make or break chemical bonds ...

  Molecules crashing into each other with tremendous force;
  atoms flying apart and rearranging themselves into new forms.

Heat does this,
or physical force such as a sharp blow—
burn the wood;
destroy the chair.

But love can be a furnace,
and heartbreak can be sharper than an axe.

So if I tell you that every time I sit on this chair I think of my
    daughter,
you understand how the chair holds my daughter within it,
how it has rearranged itself into her shape.
These few sticks of wood.

This asteroid.

   Beat.

There's this girl on the page.
Not a girl, sorry—
a young woman.

Why do we always do that?
Girls … chicks …
Why do we buy into that?
Why do I?
If she's a chick, that makes me a chook.

There's this woman.

If she's honest,
she knows her relationship is over.
Things have been falling apart for a long time.
But there are ways of doing things,
ways to behave.

After she and her boyfriend divvy everything up,
he returns to give back every gift she's ever given him.
Five years they were together,
and he gives her back every single thing.

She says she doesn't have room for all his stuff.
Does she mean in the house,
or in her heart?

The following week
she's back online getting rid of every book he gave her,
trashing each one as she goes.
Terrible books—
he clearly had terrible taste—
and these are revenge reviews of beautiful, brutal honesty.

Then there's the woman who buys a gorgeous wedding dress for
     her big day,
but when she gets it home and tries it on,
it doesn't sit right.
So she buys another one,
but that doesn't sit right either.
Which is when she realises the dress isn't the problem,
it's the bloke.
He just doesn't sit right.

And the woman with a three-D printed model of her ex-lover's
     brain,
taken from an MRI.

          I don't like it. I don't want it. Someone please take it away.

It was tiny!
A tiny little brain.

Why not just chuck it in the bin, you ask?
Because: landfill.
And landfill won't give you a bag of lemons,
a bucket of sympathy
or an offer to burn your cursed item on a pyre while chanting pagan
     spells.

People keep breaking up.
And Rough Trade keeps offering up the goods.

When it comes to relationships,
I reckon we're only ever operating on a fraction of the available
    information—
fifty per cent at best.

At best.

What do you really know about the person sharing your bed?
Your life?
Only what they tell you,
only what you see.
But these are limited tools, aren't they?
Blunt.
Your eyes can't magnify to the level of the atom
and see what's moving around inside that person—
what chemicals are bonding to each other,
or tearing each other apart.
It's why we all laughed at that joke a couple of years ago,
about hindsight being twenty-twenty vision.
It's true.
Most of the time we're stumbling around in the dark,
bumping into furniture and hoping for the best.
Sometimes you don't *want* to turn on the lights.

Well, I had the lights turned on *for* me.
So bright they blinded me for a while.

SEE WHAT YOU MADE ME DO?!

Daughter sat there in that little chair,
looking up at us,
clinging to the edge of the seat like a life raft.

What are those bruises, people asked.
I told them I'd bumped into the furniture.
Old-school.

    Beat.

Every relationship involves a trade-off,
some kind of deal.
I thought I knew what mine was.

You follow your career dreams while I take care of the kids, the
    house, all that—
still working mind you,
but jobbing,
not dreaming.
Then when they're older, I get my turn.
And in the end, they go off to do their own thing and we take care
    of each other.

Idiot.

I thought we were solid,
but I had no idea his atoms were moving in a whole other direction.
When that final blow came it was a hard, brute force.

I see now the deal was more of a Faustian pact.
The devil always gets his pound of flesh
and I didn't realise the devil thought I'd already had the good part.

It goes without saying the devil is a man.

You don't run away in the middle of the night carrying a chair.
You wait,
and try,
and plead,
and plan.
Attempt to salvage what you can.

Ripping shreds off my skin week after week on a therapist's couch.
Ripping shreds off each other.
When finally,
raw and bleeding,
I said I'd had enough,
his mates blamed me for pulling the pin on the relationship.
Only because he kept pulling it out and putting it back in again.

Only because you can't live with someone holding a hand grenade,
wondering when you might have to pick shrapnel out of your face.

I had to get rid of the wreckage of half a lifetime,
baggage we'd carried around for decades because
'it'll come in handy one day'.

That's how I discovered Rough Trade.

'Please, somebody take this stuff away from me. Trade for twenty-
one years of my life back.'

Why do we do this to ourselves?
Make ourselves vulnerable to this pain?

For a momentary brush with luck and joy?

> *Beat.*

> *She sits on the chair.*

The kids are older now.
And what they don't know, they don't have to know.
They don't need to see this.
I just tell them my housemates are pigs and the kitchen's a mess,
let's meet at a café—my shout!

They're going to love my tiny house.

SEVEN: MATTER OUT OF PLACE

She checks her phone. Nothing.

WOMAN: The page has gone quiet …

No ping, no offers.

I wrote the post badly, I wasn't funny enough, in fact I was dull.

Actively dull.

And that stupid mistake with no trade instead of name your trade
and then the edit would have screwed with the algorithm …

There's a spiralling effect, you know?
Once it's slipped down the page
and people have moved on to the cute pictures of someone's ferret …

Or maybe I've misread the room.
Maybe self-love isn't actually the new cheese fondue.

    Her phone pings.

Ooh!

> In search of horns. Boat horns, truck horns, air horns, fog
> horns. I need all kinds of horns, including the ones off
> old cars that go ah-oooga! If it starts thin and flares out
> exponentially then I'm your guy. Lizard pic for attention.

    Beat.

I'm always surprised there aren't more people in search of love.

I guess love sometimes comes in disguise,
like a stranger picking up slugs in your garden.
It's not stop-a-bus-love, or run-into-a-burning-house-love, or even
    pay-the-rent-love.
But it is love.

We are planets looking for a sun to orbit around.
It's not in our nature to be sent off spinning into the atmosphere,
untethered and alone.

    Beat.

I think the main reason we all hate slugs is that they have the
temerity to wear their slime on the outside of their bodies.

I did some more research.
If you can get past the slime,
and the fact that they sometimes turn to cannibalism,
which could obviously be a bit awkward during the sex thing—
'I could eat you up' takes on a whole new meaning—
if you can get past that,
it turns out they're pretty handy little buggers.

'Cause they eat shit.

Dead and rotting plants, fallen fruit, animal droppings, carrion, toadstools.
If they happen to munch on a leaf it's probably already diseased.

The point is, they're scavengers.
Which is exactly what Roughies are at heart.
We pick up old crap and look at it anew.

Most people get rid of stuff they don't find useful anymore,
sweep it out the door like dirt.
But dirt is just matter out of place.
If you're in the wrong tent at the races it's horse poo on your stilettos,
if you're a flower it's brunch.

Everything is a question of where you stand,
and what you put at the centre.

What happens if you take yourself out of the middle, and centre the dirt?

That's how I think of myself.
As matter out of place.

I used to have this designer coat,
full-length red suede with a plush fur collar that everyone wanted
    to stroke.
Hands constantly reaching out to me.
It was a *coat* you couldn't wear out in the rain.

In the op shop of life, we're all second-hand goods.
Once you know where you are you understand the rules.
You have to trawl through the racks,
try on a bunch of weird shit,
and if you're really lucky you might find something that's
    surprisingly perfect,
just don't look at the hole in the seam.

It's a bit like Tinder.
Minus the slugs.

For the record, I don't hate men.
Far from it.
I love them.
I love their strength, their humour, their brains, their bodies.
Give me a man with strong arms, kind eyes and a big heart
and I'm hooked.
If you're one of those men and you'd like to discuss this topic
    further, please see me after the show.
Glass of rosé thanks.

So it's not men I hate.

But … the way the patriarchy dovetails with capitalism and
    ecological destruction …
it's all part of the same scam, isn't it?

That guy I told you about who traded a wheel of cheese for a car?
His local deli was closing down and he'd bought the cheese—
this gigantic round of parmesan—
because he couldn't bear to see it go to waste.
Great idea.
I asked him,
weren't you worried you'd end up with a hunk of stinking cheese in
    the middle of your living room?
No, he said.
I figured things would all work out in the end.

But what about the day they don't?

Things don't always work out do they,
not for everyone.
I'm not blaming Cheese Guy,
not saying that men always have it easy.
But some of us get a great story to share down the pub while others
    get …
    Beat.
Others get a raw fucking deal.

That's what scares me.

I know I look a bit silly,
all this stuff back and forth,
lemons, boxes …
I know …
I'm just here,
trying to stitch up the wounds one trade at a time,
keep the wolves from the door.

Trying to find the centre.

And I've got things that glisten in the garden.

But if the page goes down again …
or I lose my phone …
the necklace breaks.

The centre cannot hold.

I call it peace, but peace is relative to war.
A thing to survive.
Otherwise you'd call it living.

> *A moment.*

Oh hell …

> *Types into her phone.*

>> Hey, are you still looking for a little chair?

Just sticks of wood, eh?

A life raft tethered to the ship of my former self.

> *She makes up one of the cardboard boxes and places the chair inside.*

Okay, little slugs.
Looks like it's you, me, and the knives.

Nobody can see us now.

> *Her phone pings.*

Oh hang on.

Attention on the phone. The light shining on her face.

Ha!

A person in Newtown has found an enormous dildo costume and is on their way over.

What do they want in return?

A lemon and a smattering of applause.

I think we can manage that.

Blackout.

THE END

JOY MINTER
AND SYDNEY FRINGE FESTIVAL

present

ROUGH TRADE

6–16 SEPTEMBER 2022

SEYMOUR CENTRE / RIVERSIDE THEATRES PARRAMATTA

Writer and performer
Katie Pollock

Director
Anthony Skuse

Producer
Joy Minter

Assistant producer
Tabitha Woo

Lighting designer
James Wallis

Sound designer
Cluny Edwards

Stage manager
Maya Soni

SUPPORTED BY

CITY OF SYDNEY

Funded by

INNER WEST

SYDNEY FRINGE FESTIVAL
1–30 SEPTEMBER 2022

PLAYWRIGHT'S NOTE

Where does a play start?

Does it start one Saturday morning in the late '70s, watching TV? The black and white Saturdays of my childhood were spent glued to the show *Swap Shop*. Actually it was called *Multi-Coloured Swap Shop* but colour TVs were what cool kids had. Kids like those on the show who had gear that other cool kids might want to trade for. Cool stuff winging its way across England. I could only watch in awe.

Does it start one Saturday night in the late '80s, in a Mini Van hurtling up the M3 to London? My then-boyfriend and I would load up his van with clothes left over from jumble sales, buy tobacco and Rizlas, and park under the Embankment, where many of the city's homeless would sleep. We offered very little—clothes, smokes and conversation—and every week I left filled with stories of life's twists and turns, series of small incidents that added up to a concrete bed. 'I didn't think this would be me,' some of them said. 'It could be you.'

Does it start on a Thursday afternoon in New York in 2014, watching a musical called *Found*? *Found* was based on a series of magazines about discarded notes, found by real people, 'celebrating the weirdness in all of us'. You can create a musical out of scraps of paper on the street?

Does it start in an agony column, 'Dear Sugar', in which Cheryl Strayed advises an angsty young woman: 'Writing is hard for every last one of us … Coal mining is harder. Do you think miners stand around all day talking about how hard it is to mine for coal? They do not. They simply dig.' The columns became a book, *Tiny Beautiful Things*, which was adapted into a play. You can make a play out of a stack of advice columns?

In 2018 I thought a lot about the idea of failure. I went to a seminar called 'How to Fail' and found myself competing to be the biggest fuck-up of the class. I wrote potential play titles in my notebook—*Things Falls Apart* (brilliant, already taken), or *Tragedy and Everything Else* (hanging onto that).

Or does it start with a trade? Rough Trade, the Facebook group, that has given me hours of laughter, along with all the stuff collected or taken away. During 2021, I interviewed people from the group. I traded them coffee and a cake in return for their time. I got fat on cake and stories.

Then I started writing. I really did want this play to be a musical (singing, dancing dildos!), but it refused to form itself into that shape. Sydney Fringe gave me an Art in Isolation residency, in which I was supposed to workshop the first draft of the play with actors. But Covid happened (again) and I couldn't get my shit together. So it ended up as just me in the theatre and those hundreds of disparate characters I was imagining all melded into one—this woman who is one small incident away from a concrete bed.

Women over 55 are the fastest growing group of people experiencing homelessness in Australia. The reasons are systemic, but that doesn't mean they can't change. This play is part of a soft revolution of people standing up to say there are other ways to do things. So maybe it starts here, one Tuesday night in September.

—Katie Pollock, 2022

DIRECTOR'S NOTE

The life-writer must explore and understand the gap between the outer self ('the fictitious V.W. whom I carry like a mask about the world') and the secret self.

—Hermione Lee, *Virginia Woolf*

The woman in *Rough Trade* may be a fictionalised version of the playwright. If the character is not what Woolf might identify as the playwright's 'outer self', then it is a fiction of that fiction. She talks to us in a conversational manner, actively constructing her narrative while masking a deeper 'secret self'. The anecdotes, and the humour, could be seen as weapons to keep us at bay or as a thread she unwinds to lead us to a deeper understanding of her and her search for a place in the order of things. She pays constant attention to her phone so not to miss the ideal trade, as if random traded objects reassure her that she is still alive. She continually re-assesses herself and her place in the world, using the subject pronoun to either question or assert the self—I know, I imagine, I am. She's fighting against the experience of becoming invisible and irrelevant in a society whose values no longer align with hers. 'Sometimes it feels pretty close to not being anything,' she says.

The woman's experience of displacement is the result of trauma that is both personal and global. Her increasing sense of isolation brought about by a marriage breakup and the subsequent shattering of expectations is compounded by living through the Covid pandemic. Once again playwright and character shadow themselves. Not only is she negotiating a patriarchal structure that allows her little agency and no power, but the very contact she craves is forbidden and dangerous.

Pollock's interest in the way trauma resonates in the body links *Rough Trade* to her earlier play *Normal*. In *Normal*, the girls' trauma was manifest in physical convulsions necessarily experienced by the actors performing them. *Rough Trade* is slyer and the trauma less obvious. Her desire 'to feel the edges of her skin' speaks not only to her emotional vulnerability, but to her actual vulnerability as an older woman facing unemployment and homelessness. Objects are her salve and her anchor. They anchor her to the here-and-now, 'one trade at a time', and to the past, 'to the ship of my former self'. That is her double bind. She will need to utilise her intelligence, her resourcefulness and her humour to redefine herself as singular and complete.

—Anthony Skuse, 2022

KATIE POLLOCK
PLAYWRIGHT / PERFORMER

Katie is an award-winning writer for stage, radio and screen. Her plays for theatre are *Normal* (Uncertainty Principle/Old 505, Canberra Youth Theatre, Hunter Drama); *The Becoming* (Redline Productions, New Theatre); *The Hansard Monologues—Age of Entitlement* (Seymour Centre/Museum of Australian Democracy/Merrigong Theatre Company/Glen St Theatre); *Blue Italian/Nil by Sea* (The Street, Apocalypse Theatre, Site & Sound Festival); *The Hansard Monologues—A Matter of Public Importance* (Seymour Centre/Merrigong Theatre Company/Casula Powerhouse/Museum of Australian Democracy); *The Blue Angel Hotel* (Tamarama Rock Surfers); *A Quiet Night in Rangoon* (subtlenuance/New Theatre); *A Girl Called Red* (Newtown Theatre); and numerous short works, including as part of *The Curve* (with Vanessa Bates, Mary Rachel Brown, Suzie Miller and Lachlan Philpott, produced by Critical Stages).

Her works for radio are *Beetroot: A bloody journey through roots and belonging* (ABC Radio National); *Nil by Sea* (ABC Radio National); *Contact* (Eastside FM); *O is for Oxygen* (Eastside FM); and *Blue Italian* (ABC Radio National). She is adapting *Normal* for film and has several TV and theatre works in development.

Awards include the Rodney Seaborn Playwrights Award, the Martin Lysicrates Prize, the Inscription/Edward Albee Playwriting Scholarship, the inaugural Town Hall Theatre 'Ingenious' award (USA), and three AWGIE nominations.

Katie also works as a dramaturg, editor and producer, has been a journalist in Australia, the UK and Thailand, was a narrative writer at the Royal Commission into Institutional Responses to Child Sexual Abuse, and is a proud member of the Australian Writers' Guild.

Normal and *The Curve* are published by Currency Press. Other plays are available at Australian Plays Transform. See: katiepollock.com

ANTHONY SKUSE
DIRECTOR

Anthony's directing credits include: *Breaking the Code* (New Theatre); Lorca's *Yerma* (AFTT, Belvoir Upstairs); Alistair McDowall's *Pomona*, (KXT, Secret House); *Love For Love* (ACA); *Three Sisters* (AFTT, Belvoir Downstairs); Katie Pollock's *Normal* (Uncertainty Principle); Jen Silverman's *Bones at the Gate* (AFTT, Belvoir Downstairs); *Crime and Punishment* (Secret House); *The Street of Crocodiles* (AFTT, Belvoir Downstairs); Joanna Erskine's *Air* (Old 505); Chekhov's *Seagull* (Secret House); Chekhov's *Play Without a Title* (AFTT, Belvoir Downstairs); Simon Stephens' *Birdland* (New Theatre); Sarah Kane's *4.48 Psychosis* (Old Fitz); Simon Stephens' *Herons* (ISA); Suzie Miller's *Sunset Strip* (Uncertainty Principle/Griffin/Critical Stages National Tour); Melita Rowston's *Between the Streetlight and the Moon* (KXT, Mophead Productions); Bathsheba Doran's *Mystery of Love and Sex* (Darlinghurst Theatre); Charlotte Jones' *Airswimming* (The Vaults, London); Tadeusz Słobodzianek's *Our Class* (AFTT, Belvoir Downstairs); Nick Enright's *Man With Five Children* (Darlinghurst Theatre Company); Katy Warner's *Dropped* (Old Fitz); Christopher Harley's *Blood Bank* (Ensemble Theatre); Jane Bodie's *Fourplay & Ride* (Darlinghurst Theatre Company); José Rivera's *The House of Ramon Iglesia* (MopHead Productions); Suzie Miller's *Caress/Ache* (Griffin); Jessica Bellamy's *Shabbat Dinner* (Rock Surfers, Rocks Pop Up Festival, Griffin); Chekhov's *Platonov* (ATYP Selects); Nick Payne's *Constellations* (Darlinghurst Theatre); Diana Son's *Stop Kiss* (Unlikely Productions); *Bite Me* (ATYP); Simon Stephens' *On the shore of the wide world* (Griffin Independent); Amy Hertzog's *4000 Miles* (Under the Wharf, Sydney, La Boite, Brisbane, Critical Stages Tour); Stephens' *Punk Rock* (Under the Wharf, three Sydney Theatre Awards including *Best Independent Production* and *Best Direction)*; Tracy Lett's *Bug*, Rivera's *References to Salvador Dali Make Me Hot,*

Marius Von Mayenburg's *The Cold Child,* Michael Gow's *Live Acts On Stage* (Griffin Independent); Mark Ravenhill's *pool (no water),* The Presnyakov Brothers' *Terrorism* (Darlinghurst Theatre Sydney).

Anthony is Head of Performance at Actors Centre Australia. He was Associate Lecturer for Performance Practices at NIDA from 2009 to 2012.

Training: Drama Studio Sydney. In 1997 and 2001 he worked with Javanese Movement Practitioner Suprapto Suryodarmo.

JOY MINTER
PRODUCER

Joy Minter worked for seven years reviewing theatre and art in Sydney, writing and editing thebuzzfromsydney, which she began in 2013, and as a contributing reviewer with the Sydney Arts Guide. When Covid shut down the theatres, she came back not as a reviewer but a producer of new Australian drama. Passionate about new writing, she co-founded the Silver Gull Writing Award with subtlenuance in 2014 and still acts as a judge of that award, which is now run by the New Theatre. This exposure to so many new and exciting plays led Joy to branch into producing, beginning in 2022 with *Son of Byblos* by James Elazzi at Belvoir 25A (co-produced with Brave New Word), followed by *Rough Trade* by Katie Pollock, debuting at the Sydney Fringe in September 2022. Joy's goal is to tell original stories that possess both heart and humour, stories that in the past have been relegated to the margins, and place these stories centre stage.

TABITHA WOO
ASSISTANT PRODUCER

Tabitha's offbeat and playful approach to theatre-making has seen her through many roles off and on stage. In addition to producing her own work, she produced the Australian premiere of *Leaves* (Some Company), *I Hate You My Mother* (assistant producer, Real Harpy/White Box Theatre with Red Line Productions) and *MinusOneSister* (assistant producer, Stories Like These for Griffin Independent). Her writing includes *Duckpond* (Old 505 FreshWorks FEMME), *House on Fire* (Old 505 Rapid Reads) and the semi-autobiographical one-woman show, *A Westerner's Guide to the Opium Wars* (Kings Cross Theatre, Sydney/The Blue Room Theatre, Perth). As an actor, Tabitha has performed with Ninefold Ensemble, Pinchgut Opera and with many writers and directors in new work development. She was part of the inaugural 2018 KXT bAKEHOUSE Step Up Team and is the founder of independent theatre company Thirty Five Square. She has a Bachelor of Performance from the Australian Institute of Music (Dramatic Arts).

JAMES WALLIS
LIGHTING DESIGNER

Originally from the UK, James is a freelance lighting designer based in Sydney. Recently James designed *Bonnie & Clyde* for JRP at The Hayes, as well as Todd McKenny and Nancye Hayes' *Casting Couch* and the David Williamson event at the Ensemble Theatre, and *The City*, a physical theatre piece at The Sydney Opera House. James was the Associate Designer on the award-winning production of *American Psycho* at the Hayes Theatre and Sydney Opera House. Other selected credits include *The Mystery of Edwin Drood* and *NINE* for Little Triangle, the opera *Love Burns* for The Other Theatre Company; the Hayes Theatre productions of *Hayes at The Hayes*, and *Siblingship* and was the Associate Designer for Red Line's *A View From The Bridge* at the Ensemble Theatre. James designed premiers of *Ugly Love* at FlightPath Theatre and the developmental production of the new Australian work *The Dismissal* for Squabbalogic.

CLUNY EDWARDS
SOUND DESIGNER

Cluny studied Music and Drama at the Arts Educational School in London. He played in various bands in the UK, where he had a publishing and recording contract as a singer/songwriter. He later established a recording studio in France, where he wrote and produced music for advertising, theatre and film. He composed *Ni Ange Ni Bete*, a musical performed at the Casino de Paris in association with the French Aids Association and *Jerusalem* a musical performed at the Sadie Bronfman Centre, Montreal, Canada. Cluny has also written and produced advertising soundtracks for Ford Europe, Radio France and Heli-Air Monaco. After moving to Australia he has continued to work on an eclectic mix of projects, including previous plays by Katie Pollock *The Blue Angel Hotel* (Old Fitzroy Theatre), *Contact* (Eastside FM) and *Basketcase* (Eastside FM).

MAYA SONI
STAGE MANAGER

Maya is a freelance performer and maker who enjoys the challenge of working in multidisciplinary settings. Maya graduated with a Bachelor of Performing Arts (Performance Making) from the Western Australian Academy of Performing Arts (WAAPA) and her practice and interest spans across acting, writing, film stunt training, musical theatre, visual arts, film-making, and backstage management. Now based in Sydney, Maya enjoys working on projects that pique her curiosity and encourage opportunities for creative challenges. Maya's previous theatre credits include; *Rabbit Punch* (Rebecca Riggs-Bennett & Company/PICA), *Here Now: Stripped Bear* (WAAPA), *The Augmented* (Spare Parts Puppet Theatre), *Wild Cherries* (WAAPA) and *Caught in A Carton* (The Blue Room Theatre). Her previous backstage credits include: *Elliot's Big Nose and the Snot That It Grows* (State Theatre Centre of WA/Perth Fringe Festival), *Threshold* (The Blue Room Theatre), *TILT* (WAAPA) and *Radiant Vermin* (Studio Sputnik).

WITH THANKS

I gratefully acknowledge the support of Sydney Fringe Festival through its Art in Isolation and Made in Sydney programs, the Inner West Council and the City of Sydney.

A huge thanks to the members and moderators of Rough Trade Sydney Facebook group—you are hilarious and I am forever in your debt.

Thanks also to: Merrigong Theatre Company for hosting the first showing of this work through its Made from Scratch program; Callum McLean and Karolina Ristevski for early audience support and kind words; Sophia Davidson Gluyas for the writing jams, the dramaturgy and the love; Joy Minter for believing in me and this project; Charley Sanders for producing mentoring and app writing genius; Peter Matheson for structure thoughts; Actors Centre Australia for space; Kate Gaul for facilitating connections; James Balian for videos, photos and always being on team; Roger Vickery for calm advice; Kerri Glasscock and Peta Downes for everything you've done to support this work; Cecilia Morrow for being me; Jacqui Reid for the chairs; Peter Troy Wojtowicz for welcoming me into your home; Sarah Christopher for flying halfway around the world to support your sister; Jude Bowler, Suzi Dougherty, Merridy Eastman, Suzie Miller and Katrina Van Stom for all your love and friendship—the most amazing friends I could ask for; Claire Grady and my fantastic colleagues at Currency Press; and Anthony Skuse for your love and care, and your love and care of new plays—thank you for everything. **KP**

SYDNEY FRINGE FESTIVAL

AUGUST & SEPTEMBER 2022

FRINGE IS BACK!

SYDNEY STORIES
ALL SEPTEMBER

www.ingramcontent.com/pod-product-compliance
Lightning Source LLC
Chambersburg PA
CBHW050027090426
42734CB00021B/3456